# MONSTER RANCH
## Feathers of Fear

Written by Sarah Allen

Illustrated by Ash Roy

# Collins

# Chapter 1

Have you ever felt like there was something hiding under your bed? Ever worried about a monster reaching up and grabbing your uncovered foot?

Well, I'm here to tell you that you have nothing to worry about.

There are zero monsters under your bed. I promise.

They're under mine.

I'm Gabby Amelia Penrose, the world-famous
monster wrangler. And that's a good thing, because
the entrance to Monster Ranch, where all the monsters come
from, is under my bed.

"Gabby!" Mum called from the front room.
"I'm heading out!"

I could barely hear her without my hearing aids, so I quickly
put them in and got out of bed.

Mum stood by the front door in her hiking boots. Mum is an expert hiker and rock climber. Because I have Turner Syndrome, I had to have heart surgery when I was born, so hiking and rock climbing aren't the easiest things for me. But that's OK; Mum brings me back cool rocks that she finds, and I wrangle all the monsters.

"I'll be back tonight," Mum said.

"Climb safe," Dad said.

Mum walked out of the door, and Dad nudged my shoulder. "Just you and me today, eh?" he said. "I'm going to work in my studio for a while and then how about we go and get some ice cream?"

Dad's a painter. Sometimes I'm sad that I can't paint like he does, but I love seeing all the beautiful things he makes.

"Sounds perfect!" I said.

I hurried to my room and got dressed. But I'd barely put on my favourite purple T-shirt before Dad called my name.

"Gabby!" he said. "Come here for a second."

I rushed to Dad's studio. He was holding up his glasses.
He uses them when he paints. "Look at this," he said.

Dad's glasses were all scraped, scratched and bent.
Like something with a big sharp beak had been pecking
at them.

Something monstrous.

# Chapter 2

"Do you think there's another monster on the loose?"
Dad asked.

I gasped. "I forgot to check under my bed this morning!"

I dashed to my bedroom and peeked under my bed.
That's when I saw it – a long, black feather, shiny and oily,
with a glowing green tip.

A monster feather of fear!

It was time to investigate.

I put the feather in my Monster Wrangling Backpack and went back to Dad's studio.

"Looks like it wasn't just my glasses," Dad said. "My gold paint is missing too."

"Uh oh," I said.

The doorbell rang, and I hurried to the door. It was our neighbour, Mr Brooks. He wore trouser braces and bow ties and had curly white hair. Normally, he had a big smile on his face, but not today.

"Hello," he said. "I'm stopping by with a question. Have either of you seen my gold watch? I might have dropped it on one of my walks. It was a present from my wife, from the very first trip we took together to New York City. It's quite precious to me."

"I haven't seen anything," said Dad. "But we'll keep our eyes open, won't we, Gabby Gabs?"

I nodded. "There's a monster on the loose. It stole my dad's paint, and it might have stolen your watch, too."

"Oh dear!" exclaimed Mr Brooks.

"Don't worry," I said. "I'll do my utmost to find it.
I'm an expert monster wrangler!"

"Utmost is a good word," said Mr Brooks. "And I'm sure
you will."

Mr Brooks said goodbye, and in a flash, I was ready.

"I'm going tracking," I told Dad.

"Stay in the neighbourhood," he replied.

I hurried out of the door. "Where to start?"

Then the first clue fell out of the sky.

A feather. A black-and-green monster feather.

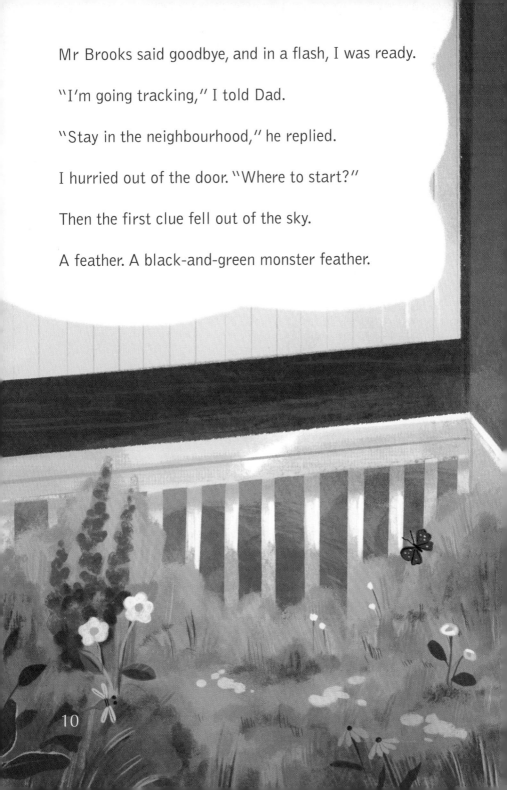

# Chapter 3

I chased the feather as it drifted
in the wind. It was black with
a shiny green tip.

"A perfect match," I said. I grabbed
it and added it to my backpack.

There, under the bushes ...

"Another feather!"

There was another feather down the street caught in
the gutter. Then another after that, and another.

Soon I'd followed black monster feathers around the block
and down the street to the local park. The park I came to
sometimes to ride the swings.

The feathers led right to the tunnel.

I paused. I listened carefully.
But even with hearing aids,
I still don't hear perfectly.

So, I crept closer. I peeked into
the tunnel ...

13

There, right in the middle, was the monster.

She had a head like a bird, with a crown full of those black-and-green feathers. Her body was long and scaly like a lizard. Or a dragon.

"Hello there," I said.

The monster looked at me with
shiny eyes. Her feathers ruffled,
and I realised she was sitting
on something. A pile of somethings, all
golden and sparkly. There were coins
and jewellery and shiny decorations.
There was Mr Brooks' watch!
And there was Dad's gold paint!

"So you like shiny, golden things,
do you?"

The monster made a little squawk.

"Well, I'm sorry, but these don't
belong to you." I reached towards
the monster's pile. I should have
known better, because all I managed
to reach was Dad's paint before
the monster gave me a sharp peck on
the hand.

"Ouch!" I said, shaking my fingers.
I sighed. "What am I going to do
about you?"

# Chapter 4

I paced back and forth in front of the tunnel. What did
I know about this monster? Mostly, I knew she collected gold,
shiny things.

I looked at Dad's tube of paint in my hand. "Aha!" I said.
"I know what to do!"

I ran home, Dad's paint in my pocket. Quickly, I took out my
box of Mum's hiking rocks.

"Get ready to be monster bait," I told them.

I carried the rocks to Dad's studio. Even though my finger coordination isn't so great, and even though I can't paint the way my dad does, I hoped my idea would still work.

I got a big brush from the drawer and began painting. Soon all the rocks were glittering and gold. It was a bit messy, and my fingers were gold-splattered too, but the job was done.

Then, as fast as I could, I carried the rocks back to the playground.

The monster was still in her tunnel, guarding her stash.

Slowly, I laid down a golden rock at the edge of the playground, right where she could see it.

"Come on, girl, look at these pretty golden treasures," I said.

*Please let this work*, I thought.

# Chapter 5

First, the monster just stared.
She ruffled her feathers, always
keeping her eye on the gold. Then she
stood, stretched, and lumbered
towards the rock. She picked it up
with one bird-like claw and stuffed it
into a scaly pouch on her belly.

"That's right," I said. "Good girl."

I laid down the next rock. The monster followed.

"Yes!" I whispered. "It's working!"

I laid down another rock, then another. Soon, the monster was striding behind me, collecting each golden rock.

The monster followed me, collecting rocks, all the way out of the park and down the street. We reached my house, and she followed me inside. Finally, I led the monster through the door into my room. The monster's talons clicked on the floor.

I tossed the last golden rock under the bed. "There it is, see?"
I said. "Time to go home."

The monster squawked. She ducked, and waddled under
the bed. A shadow opened up, and then the monster was gone.

# Chapter 6

I ran back to the park. For the rest of the day, I brought the monster's golden trinkets back to where they belonged.

"Oh, thank you, Gabby!" said Mr Brooks. "I'm so happy to have my watch back. You really are an expert monster wrangler!"

That night, while Mum got my daily injection ready, I told her and Dad all about how I wrangled the monster. "Even though I can't paint as well as you," I said, "it still worked!"

Dad smiled. "You don't have to paint like anyone else to be a smart, effective painter," he said. "Good work!"

"Ready?" Mum said, holding the needle.

"Yep!" I said. "It's better than getting pecked by a monster!"

# A thank-you letter

Dear Gabby,

Thank you again for returning my gold watch. I'll always remember the moment you did — 4:17 pm! My wife bought this watch for me on our very first trip to New York. It was a reminder of our time visiting our favourite art museums. Now we are back visiting again, and we found the same shop where she bought the watch! I hope you enjoy this postcard and picture, as well as this necklace, as a token of our appreciation. If New York City ever has monster troubles, I know who they should call!

Happy monster hunting!

Your neighbour,

Mr Brooks

#  Ideas for reading

Written by Christine Whitney
*Primary Literacy Consultant*

**Reading objectives:**
- discuss words and phrases that capture the reader's interest and imagination
- check that the text makes sense to them, discuss their understanding and the meaning of words in context
- draw inferences such as inferring characters' feelings, thoughts and motives from their actions
- predict what might happen from details stated and implied
- identify main ideas drawn from more than one paragraph and summarising these

**Spoken language objectives:**
- participate in discussions
- speculate, hypothesise, imagine and explore ideas through talk
- ask relevant questions

**Curriculum links:** PSHE education – learn to recognise the ways in which they are the same and different to others

**Interest words:** ranch, wrangler, utmost, lumbered, appreciation

## Build a context for reading
- Before looking at the book, encourage children to share their understanding of the words *ranch* and *wrangler*. Make connections with the other Monster Ranch book, *Paws of Doom*, where appropriate.
- Look at the title on the front cover, then closely at the illustration. Discuss where this story might be set and make predictions as to what the story will be about. What are the characters doing on the front cover? What clue is there that explains why this book is called a fantasy story?
- Read the blurb on the back cover and look again at the illustration of Gabby on the front cover. Ask children to suggest how she might try to capture the monster.

## Understand and apply reading strategies
- Read Chapter 1 together. Summarise what the reader knows about Gabby by the end of the chapter.
- Continue to read together up to the end of Chapter 2. Gabby says to Mr Brooks that she will do her *utmost* to find his watch. Ask children to suggest another word or phrase that means the same as *utmost*.